WE'RE TALKING ABOUT
DISABILITY

JENNY BRYAN

WAYLAND

Editor: Carron Brown
Designer: John Christopher
Consultant: Nick Tapp, assistant organizer and information officer,
East Sussex Association for the Disabled

First published in 1996 by Wayland Publishers Ltd
61 Western Road, Hove, East Sussex, BN3 1JD, England

British Library Cataloguing in Publication Data

Bryan, Jenny
We're Talking About Disability
I. TITLE
362.4
ISBN 0-7502-1862-2

Typeset by White Design, England
Printed and bound by Canale & C.S.p.A., Turin, Italy

Picture Acknowledgements
Angus Blackburn cover, APM Studios title page, 4 (top and bottom),
5 (top and bottom), 10–19; Eye Ubiquitous 8, 21, 22; Allan Flachs 20,
Sally & Richard Greenhill 6, 7, 9, 23, 28; Popperfoto 26, 27; Science
Photo Library 24, 25; Wayland Picture Library 29.

Wayland Publishers Ltd would like to thank the children of
Blatchington Mill School and Patcham House Day Special School.
Most of the people who are photographed in this book are models.

Contents

Meet Cathy, Mark, Nicky and Michael 4

Why are some people disabled? 6

Cathy can't see very well 10

Michael can't hear well 12

Michael and his friends 14

People in wheelchairs need access 16

'I need a little extra help' 18

How would you manage? 20

Making life easier 22

Living with disability 24

Getting help 28

Glossary 30

Index 32

Meet Cathy, Mark, Nicky and Michael

Cathy, Mark, Nicky and Michael are about your age. They live at home with their families and they go to schools like yours.

Cathy is horse mad; she goes riding every Saturday and likes to help out at the stable after her lesson. She can tell you about every type of bit and bridle.

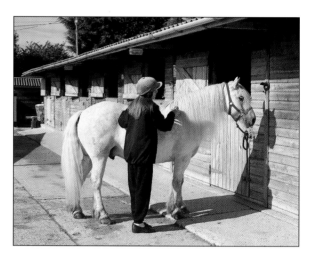

▲ Cathy

▲ Michael

Michael supports Manchester United football team and goes to as many of their matches as he can. He's quite good at football himself and plays for the school team. Last season he scored more goals than anyone else and he hopes that one day he'll get to play for his favourite club.

Nicky loves to paint, and she's very good at it. Some of her pictures have been displayed inside her school, and inside her

▲ Nicky

Cathy can't see very well, and Michael can't hear very much. Mark gets about in a wheelchair as he can't move his legs, and Nicky has a learning difficulty. Their disabilities don't stop them enjoying life, and all of them want to do something exciting when they grow up.

Nicky hopes to go to art college, Michael wants to play for Manchester United. Cathy hasn't decided what she would like to do yet and Mark keeps changing his mind. Last week he thought it would be nice to work with computers.

local library. She likes to paint with bright colours best, so her pictures are always colourful.

Mark likes spending time with his friends, Andrew and Sarah. They go everywhere together and like doing lots of things. They often go shopping or watch videos at home. They also play computer games, although Mark usually wins when they play Sonic the Hedgehog.

Nicky, Mark, Michael and Cathy are good at some lessons and not at others – just like other pupils in their schools. They have extra problems sometimes because each has a disability.

▲ Mark

Why are some people disabled?

There are lots of reasons why people are physically disabled or have mental disabilities. Some people are born blind or deaf, or unable to move about or think clearly. Something may have happened in their mother's womb which stopped a vital part of their body or brain from growing properly. Taking certain drugs during pregnancy can sometimes do this, and so can drinking too much alcohol. But, often, doctors don't know why a baby is damaged while it is in the womb. It's nobody's fault.

Sometimes a baby's brain may not develop fully before birth, or just after it has been born. This is called cerebral palsy. Sometimes the cause can be found, but not always. Children with cerebral palsy can have a variety of disabilities. Sometimes these can be quite minor, but they can also be very severe.

◀ This man uses a white cane to help him find his way around, and to let people know that he is blind.

▲ Car accidents like this one can sometimes injure people very badly.

Of course, doctors do their best to make sure that babies get the best medical attention at birth. But occasionally there is a problem. For example, when a baby is born too soon, before it's fully developed, doctors may be unable to get enough oxygen to its brain, even with machines to help them. The baby's brain may become damaged in spite of all the efforts of the doctors.

Another reason people have disabilities is through accidents. Road accidents are one of the most common causes of serious disability. Nearly a quarter of a million road accidents are reported in Britain alone each year. Of these, over 300,000 people are injured, about one in five of them seriously.

Some of the seriously injured may be left paralyzed and unable to move part or all of their body, or they may lose their sight or hearing. They may need to have part or all of a limb removed because it's so badly hurt.

Being physically disabled does not necessarily mean you can't think straight. Most people who can't see or hear properly, or who use a wheelchair, can think just as clearly as you and your friends.

Accidents can also leave people with mental disabilities. They may find it hard to concentrate or remember things. In the worst cases, their brain may be so badly damaged that they can't think like they used to do. They think and act like small children.

As people get older they may get diseases such as multiple sclerosis, heart disease, arthritis or dementia, which can leave them physically or mentally disabled. Their joints may become diseased

▼ When people get older they may need someone to help care for them. This man has a carer who helps him by pushing his wheelchair.

so they can't move around very easily, or their nerves may start to wear out so they can't control their movements. If the nerves in their brain become tangled and diseased they may become confused, and find it impossible to concentrate. Then someone else has to look after them.

Doctors usually separate mental disability caused by damage to the brain, for example in the womb or in an accident, from mental health problems. People can become ill mentally in the same way as they can become ill physically. The only difference is that the disease affects their brain rather than their heart, lungs or other parts of their body.

Anxiety and depression are the most common types of mental health problems. People can become very nervous or unhappy; they may be worried about work or upset about something at home. Sometimes the problem goes away and they stop feeling anxious or depressed.

▲ Worrying too much can sometimes make you ill with anxiety.

But some people need treatment to get over their illness, just as they would need treatment for an infection or a breathing problem. Counselling is one type of treatment that people with mental health problems may receive. It allows them to talk to someone who understands their problems and will help them to work out how to cope with their illness.

Yet even with treatment, some people with severe mental health problems may not ever recover completely.

Cathy can't see very well

Cathy was born with very poor eyesight and no one really knows why. She can see bits of colour but very little more.

Since she has never been able to see very much, Cathy does not know what things look like. She has learned to feel the shape and texture of things, to judge how big they are and whether they are rough or smooth. She knows that water is wet, that the sun feels hot on her skin but she doesn't know what the sea looks like on a sunny day.

Cathy learned to ride in the same way as other children. She knows that she has to sit firmly in the saddle and grip her pony's sides with her legs to stop herself from falling off. Her pony is very steady and Cathy can make it trot and even canter around the ring, just like everyone else.

There are many different types of sight problems. Some see things rather like a jigsaw puzzle

▲ Cathy has had poor eyesight since she was born.

with two or three large pieces missing. Others have tunnel vision, so they can only see what is straight in front of them and nothing on either side.

How bad a person's eyesight is depends on what part of their eye is damaged. Light enters the eye through the dark pupil at the centre of the eyeball. It is then focused by a lens just behind the pupil on to an area at the back of the eye, called the retina.

Information about images recorded on the retina is sent along nerves to the vision centre of the brain, which then decodes the information so that you know what you are looking at.

Some people can't focus light very well and everything looks blurred unless they wear glasses. Other people have a tear on the retina and any image that lands on the damaged area can't be recorded. Tunnel vision occurs if the pressure of the fluid in the eye gets too high and interferes with the blood supply to the retina. Sometimes, the defect is in the vision centre of the brain. This means that although the eyes are undamaged, the brain can't decode the signals coming from the retina of each eye.

▲ Horseriding is Cathy's favourite hobby.

Michael can't hear well

Michael caught a serious infection, called meningitis, when he was five. It affected his brain and he lost most of his hearing. Now Michael's twelve, and he can still remember what it is like to hear clearly. Unlike Cathy, who has to imagine what her pony looks like, Michael knows what the crowd sounds like when he's watching Manchester United playing. He cheers with everyone else when his team scores a goal.

Michael has no trouble speaking because he learned to talk before his hearing became damaged. Children who are born deaf find it much harder to speak clearly because they can't imagine what words sound like, and they need help to be able to understand. There is nothing wrong with the voice box (the part of the body that helps you speak) in their throat, but they don't know how to use it.

Although Michael can speak he doesn't know how loud his voice is because he can't hear himself. A lot of deaf people have this problem. Sometimes they shout and sometimes they whisper, but they don't know they are doing it unless someone tells them.

There are several reasons why people can't hear well. You probably know someone who

◀ Michael has had a hearing problem since he was five.

can't hear sometimes because they have glue ear. This is when the middle part of their ear gets blocked with fluid, so sounds can't get through to their inner ear where they are recorded. Within the inner ear is a coiled tube, called the cochlea, which contains thousands of sensitive hair cells connected to the brain by nerves. Sounds pass through the cochlea where the hair cells pick them up, sending messages along a large nerve to the hearing centre in the brain.

Many people with hearing problems have damaged hair cells in the cochlea, which means that some sound messages don't get passed on to the brain unless they are very loud noises. These people can be helped with hearing-aids which make sounds much louder than they really are.

Unfortunately, Michael's infection caused so much damage that hearing-aids only help slightly. So, he has learned to lip-read. By looking at the shapes that the mouth makes with certain words, Michael can understand what his friends are saying. To be able to lip-read Michael must face the person who's talking so that he can see the person's mouth.

▼ In school, Michael, Simon and Chris like working together on projects.

Michael and his friends

Simon and Chris are in the same class as Michael and at times they are embarrassed to be with him. They sometimes have to repeat things several times before he understands what they are saying. When they go out, Michael often speaks in a loud voice when he gets excited and doesn't realize how noisy he's being. Simon and Chris say 'shoosh' to him, but it's usually too late and people are staring at them all.

▲ Michael doesn't like Simon and Chris leaving him out of their plans – it makes him feel sad.

When Simon and Chris go out with their other friends from school they tend not to ask Michael. They even discuss their plans in front of him because they know he can't hear them. They just make sure he can't see their mouths to lip-read what they are saying. They also make fun of his hearing problem. 'Don't tell Michael' they say to each other, and then they laugh. They think it's a great joke.

Michael may have a hearing problem but he isn't stupid. He knows when Simon and Chris and the others are talking about him or planning something. They watch him while they are talking and look away as soon as he looks at them. They talk behind their hands. Michael knows he's being left out and it makes him feel very down.

Michael's mum thinks Simon and Chris are jealous because they are not in the football team. Michael gets on with all the boys in the team but they are in the class above him and he wants friends in his own class too.

Many children with disabilities have the same problems as Michael, making friends and fitting in. It's much easier to ignore someone who has a sight or hearing problem, uses a wheelchair or has a learning disability, than it is to make the effort to help them. They are easy targets for bullies if they can't stand up for themselves.

Do you ever stare at people with disabilities – a woman with a white cane or a guide dog, a man who uses a wheelchair? We all do it. Think how you would feel if people stared at you and ignored you when you wanted help. Other people's attitudes can be one of the biggest problems disabled people face. Yet don't be offended if a disabled person turns down your offer of help; they simply may not need it.

▼ Simon and Chris wish that they were as good as Michael at football.

People in wheelchairs need access

Mark was knocked over by a car when he was eight and his spinal cord was badly damaged. He can't feel anything below his waist. He's partially paralyzed and can't walk but he can still use his arms.

How paralyzed a person is depends on where their spinal cord was damaged. Mark's was injured quite low down in his back so he is paralyzed below the waist. If the spinal cord is damaged higher up, the paralysis is much worse and affects the arms as well as the legs. For example, someone who breaks their neck, like the Superman actor Christopher Reeve, can move very little. Sometimes, they may not be able to breathe without a machine, although intensive therapy can help them make the most of the movement they have left.

▲ Mark's spinal cord was damaged when he was eight.

Mark gets around in a wheelchair. Sometimes one of his friends, Andrew or Sarah, pushes him or he can make the wheels go round himself, using his arms. His parents' house has been adapted so that he can get his wheelchair in and out easily, and the school bus has a special platform which goes up and down to help him get on board. Mark's school was given special grants to make the entrances to all the classrooms wide enough for wheelchairs and there are ramps and lifts so he does not need to use the stairs.

Going shopping with his friends can be much more difficult. Only the newest, biggest shops in town can take Mark's wheelchair. Even then, he doesn't like to go at busy times because he feels in everyone's way. People stare at him. It's almost impossible to go shopping on a Saturday, when it's really busy. So Mark, Andrew and Sarah go shopping after school, when the shops are quieter.

The counters in the shops are too high for Mark when he is sitting in his wheelchair, and it's embarrassing to have to ask for things to be brought to him. Getting clothes off rails is difficult too, and trying them on in the changing room is almost impossible. Mark usually buys clothes from shops that let him take them home to try on.

Going to the cinema is much easier since they built the new multi-screen complex. By law, all new public buildings in Britain have to be accessible to people who use wheelchairs by having ramps and lifts. If everywhere was designed like this Mark could go anywhere he wanted.

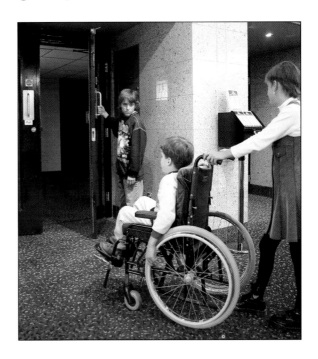

▲ Mark, Andrew and Sarah are really happy that ramps were built in the new cinema. It's now very easy for Mark to see the films he wants to see.

'I need a little extra help'

Nicky has a learning disability. Her mum noticed it when Nicky was quite young. She took longer than her older brother and sister to learn to put her clothes on and to play simple games. When she started school she found it harder to learn to read and write than the other children in her class.

▲ Nicky has always found it difficult to learn things as quickly as her friends.

Nicky's teacher saw that Nicky had a problem and talked it over with her mum. The local education department agreed that Nicky should have some extra help. For maths, English and science lessons, an assistant teacher comes into the class and sits with Nicky to help her understand what is being taught.

Several other children in the school have the same sort of extra help. Some have help for one or two classes, others for more. Some, like Nicky, need help with English and maths, others have help with history, geography or French. Each pupil gets the help he or she most needs.

Nicky enjoys the assistant teacher's help in the classroom. She wouldn't want to go into a separate room for her extra help; she likes to stay with her friends. Yet, some children with learning disabilities prefer to have their extra help out of the classroom.

▲ A special teacher gives Nicky extra help with a school project.

The other children in Nicky's class wish they were as good as Nicky at art. She's always been good at drawing pictures and she can help the other children when it's time for art. Nicky's mum enjoys coming to the open day at the school because Nicky's pictures are always on display.

People aren't so helpful when Nicky is out and about. She has trouble counting out money when she is buying something, and the shop assistants can be very impatient. If she asks them to help they sometimes snatch her money and take what they need without stopping to explain what they're doing.

Getting on the bus is the most worrying time. If she hasn't got the right money she often walks home rather than risk the sighs and groans of the bus driver. Other people don't always have the right money either but the driver doesn't seem to make such a fuss with them.

How would you manage?

Have you ever wondered what it's like to have a disability? Look at the pictures on these two pages and think about the problems that disabled people would have to deal with. On page 31 you can look up the possible problems found in both pictures, and how they could be reduced.

The picture on this page shows a street near the busy centre of a town. Look closely at the picture and write down four things that you think could cause problems for someone who couldn't see very well.

Now, think about what could be done to reduce the problems that you have spotted.

The picture on this page shows an audience in a packed theatre waiting to see a play. Look closely at the picture and write down three things that you think would help someone with a hearing problem enjoy the play as much as any other person.

Look again at the picture and think about things you can't see straight away. Write down three things that you think could cause problems for a person using a wheelchair in a theatre, and how the problems could be solved.

Making life easier

Life can be made easier in many ways for disabled people. Children like Cathy learn to read by touch using a special kind of writing called Braille. Each Braille letter is made of raised dots, arranged like the six dots on a domino. For example, the letter 'L' has three raised dots in a vertical row on the left side of the 'domino'. The letter 'P' is the same as 'L' but with an extra dot at the top of the right hand column. Blind people can use Braille typewriters to write.

Children with a little more vision than Cathy can use large-print books. Many children, and adults, find it enjoyable to listen to books on tapes, whether they can see or not.

Like Michael, children who can't hear very well learn to lip-read. You can help by speaking clearly and a little more slowly than usual. It's easier to follow what you are saying if you use complete sentences rather than words on their own. If you change the subject, pause to make it clear you are talking about something else. Don't talk behind your hands like Chris and Simon, always look at the person

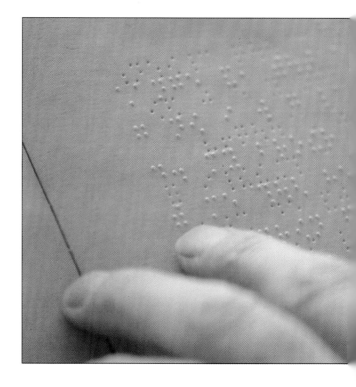

This is a page from a Braille book. ▶ All the letters are raised in a series of dots so that people with sight problems can read by touch.

▲ These children use sign language and lip-reading to understand one another.

who is lip-reading and face the light at the same time if you can.

Some children who are deaf can't speak and they use sign language instead. You can find out about sign language from one of the organizations in the 'Getting help' chapter.

For children who use a wheelchair, like Mark, the most important thing is to be able to get around easily. Although modern buildings have to be built with doorways, ramps and lifts to allow wheelchair access, many older buildings have not been converted. In the same way, new laws will insist that new buses, trains and taxis are designed for disabled people, but older vehicles will still be inaccessible for wheelchair users.

Children with learning difficulties, like Nicky, can go to ordinary schools. But people with more severe mental disabilities need specialized help, especially as they get older.

Hardly a week goes by without a piece of new equipment being invented or adapted to help disabled people.

Children like Mark can now use wheelchairs powered by electricity to help them move around. There are special controls on the side of the wheelchair that can move it left and right, forwards and backwards just with a slight movement from the user's hand. As you can imagine, having a powered wheelchair makes going up hills no problem at all.

Life can be made easier around the home with easier-living aids. These aids are basic everyday equipment that we use that have been adapted for easier use by disabled people. There are electric plugs with handles on them, so that they can be gripped more easily. For people with hearing difficulties there is a telephone extension bell, which can be taken into any room so that they can hear the telephone ringing.

There are also tap turners and key turners that attach a lever to the object making it easier to grip and turn. For those who find it difficult to reach for things there are many more adaptations to make life easier: long-handled brushes, combs, gas lighters for cookers and basic 'reachers' that can pick up even very small items from the floor. The Disabled Living Centres Council (DLCC) can give more advice on these products and can tell you where to buy them. Its

▲ This remote-controlled hearing aid can pick up sounds, making them both clearer and louder.

address can be found in the Getting Help chapter.

People with sight problems find that guide dogs can help them a lot with everyday life. Guide dogs are specially trained to help people with sight problems move around safely through shops, across roads and around the home. There are also specially trained hearing dogs that can help people with hearing problems. The dogs can tell their owners when there's someone at the door or if the telephone's ringing. The guide dogs and the hearing dogs are a huge help to their owners, and they are also great friends to have.

Some disabled people who find moving around difficult, even in the home, can use computers to make life easier and allow them to live more independently. From their chair or bed, they can use a computer to answer the door, telephone their friends, watch television

▲ This man uses a voice-controlled computer to control the lights and television in his house.

and control the temperature of their room. On top of this they can use a word processor to write letters and reports. If people have some movement in their hands or feet they can operate these systems using them. If they can't move but can speak, the computers will work with spoken commands. Unfortunately these computer systems are quite costly and not everyone can afford to buy them.

These aids are just some of the many different ways that can help make life happier, healthier and easier for disabled people.

Living with disability

Disability does not stop people from living happy and successful lives.

The blind British Member of Parliament (MP) David Blunkett speaks for the Labour party. He is often seen in the thick of a heated debate in the House of Commons with his guide dog lying calmly at his feet. For years, former Labour MP Jack Ashley campaigned tirelessly on behalf of people with disabilities while he himself was unable to hear.

American actress, Phyllis Freilich, became the best known deaf stage actress in the world in 1980 for her performance in New York in the play, 'Children of a Lesser God'. The play portrayed the relationship between a deaf student and her teacher. In the same way, the American comedian Richard Pryor has not allowed his multiple sclerosis to prevent him from performing in clubs in the USA. He simply uses a motorized wheelchair to get about.

Perhaps the most famous wheelchair user of the 1980s and 1990s is the British physicist Stephen Hawking. Much of his research on the creation of the universe has been done since he became disabled by an incurable disease of the nervous system.

◄ David Blunkett MP (far right) at the Labour Party conference.

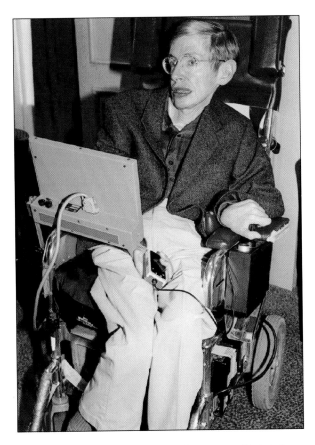

▲ Stephen Hawking, a famous British physicist.

Richard Leakey, the Kenyan wildlife specialist, did not even bother with a wheelchair when both his legs had to be amputated after a plane crash. He learned to walk with artificial legs, and his disability has not stopped him campaigning for a more democratic political system in his country.

Rather less well known but no less determined is musician Steve Knight. He was born with cerebral palsy and can't move or speak very much. Yet, in 1994, he played his own musical compositions on a bank of electronic synthesisers at a London concert hall. Knight plays the keyboard with his feet and operates the computer with his big toe.

All these people have fought to the top of their professions. But you don't have to be famous or successful to have a happy life, whether or not you have a disability. Thousands of people with disabilities lead ordinary lives just like most other people. As you have seen, they live at home and go to school like others. They grow up, get jobs and have families of their own. They don't need your pity or your embarrassment. But, from time to time, they may need you to spare a moment to help them.

Getting help

There are many organizations that people with disabilities can contact for advice, information and support. Details of local organizations working with disabled people can be found in local libraries and in the Yellow Pages under 'Disabled'.

◀ The woman on the left has had support from the RNIB.

The Royal National Institute for the Blind (RNIB) is the largest charity representing blind people. It produces booklets and tapes on many subjects such as learning and teaching Braille, and vision in the classroom. You can contact the RNIB at 224 Great Portland Street, London W1N 6AA. Tel: (0171) 388 1266.

The Royal National Institute for Deaf People (RNID) provides a similar service to that of the RNIB, for adults with hearing problems. It can be contacted at 105 Gower Street, London WC1E 6AH. Tel: (0171) 387 8033. The National Deaf Children's Society for children with hearing problems is based at 15 Dufferin Street, London EC1Y 8PD. Tel: (0171) 250 0123.

The Royal Association for Disability and Rehabilitation

▲ This woman receives help from a local organization. It helps her to visit the shops and her friends in town by giving her some access to their transport.

(RADAR) is an organization that helps people with a wide variety of disabilities, providing helpful advice and support; it also campaigns for improvements in services. Its address is Unit 12, City Forum, 250 City Road, London EC1V 8AF.
Tel: (0171) 250 3222.

Scope is Britain's largest disability charity. It helps people with cerebral palsy, their families and carers. It can be contacted at 12 Park Crescent, London W1N 4EQ. Tel: (0171) 636 5020.

The Disabled Living Centres Council (DLCC) is a national organization providing advice and information about special adapted equipment for disabled people. It can be contacted at first floor, Winchester House, 11 Cranmer Road, London SW9 6EJ.
Tel: (0171) 820 0567.

Disabled people are entitled to financial and other help from the government. To find out about disability benefits you should contact your local employment or benefits offices.

Glossary

Arthritis a painful disease in which the joints between the bones become inflamed and swollen, making movement painful.

Cerebral palsy a paralysis that affects some or all parts of the body. Sometimes caused by lack of oxygen to the brain around the time of birth.

Cochlea the part of the inner ear where sounds are recorded before they are passed on to the brain.

Dementia an illness that affects mainly elderly people, making them confused and unable to concentrate or remember things.

Implants small devices that can be inserted under the skin and left in place either deep in the body or nearer the surface.

Lens in the eye, a transparent, curved structure behind the pupil that helps to focus light on to the retina.

Meningitis a bacterial or viral infection, more common in children, which can cause damage to the brain and other organs.

Multiple sclerosis a disease in which nerves lose their protective outer coating. This prevents them from passing messages around the body, resulting in gradual paralysis.

Nerves a bundle of fibres that pass messages through the body to tell it when the body's moving or feeling something, such as heat or cold.

Paralyzed the loss of function in muscles. This leads to an inability to move.

Pupil the hole in the middle of the eye that lets the correct amount of light into the retina.

Retina the part of the eye that records images ready for decoding by the brain.

Spinal cord a long tube within the spine, containing the nerves that carry messages from the brain to the rest of the body.

Tendons the cords that attach muscles to bones.

Books to read

Children and Disability by Jean Johnstone (Daniels Publications, 1993)

Facts About: Physically Disabled (Simon & Schuster Young Books, 1991)

Let's Talk About Disabled People by Reiser and Sullivan (Franklin Watts, 1991)

Life Crisis: Disability (Heinemann's Children's Reference, 1993)

Further information about leaflets, books, tapes and videos can be obtained from the organizations mentioned on pages 28–29.

Problems and possible solutions to the pictures on pages 20-21.

Page 20: four problems and possible solutions for a person with a sight problem: 1. Busy traffic near the end of the road – should be crash barriers along the sides of busy roads to prevent people from crossing. 2. Steps jutting out into the pavement – the sides should have barriers around them to warn people that they are there. 3. Bikes leaning against walls– these bikes should be parked in the road, out of the way of pedestrians so they won't be tripped over. 4. Roadworks on the pavement and road – should have flashing lights and beepers so that pedestrians are warned about them in advance.

Page 21a: three things that will help a person with a hearing problem enjoy the play: 1. Reserved seating near the front to make lip-reading easier. 2. Electronic sub-titles placed above the stage. 3. An interpreter on the stage who can hand sign the words of the play.

Page 21b: three problems and possible solutions for a person who uses a wheelchair: 1. Narrow aisles – take out a line of seating to widen the aisles, or have a reserved, raised area for wheelchair users. 2. Steps in old theatres – should build in ramps, or a lift for access, providing an alternative route into and through the theatre. 3. Toilets may be far away from the seating area, and may even be on a different level – toilets should be built that are suitable for wheelchair users close to the entrance of the seating area.

Index

Ashley, Jack 26

blindness 6
brain, damage to 6–7, 9, 11
Braille 20, 22
Blunkett, David 26

cerebral palsy 6, 27
cochlea 13, 24
computers 25

deafness 6, 12–15, 23, 24
diseases 8

eyesight, damage to 8, 10–11, 15, 22

glue ear 13

hazards 20
hearing, damage to 6, 8, 13
hearing-aids 13, 24
Hawking, Stephen 26, 27

implants 24

Knight, Steve 27

Leakey, Richard 27
lip-reading 13, 14, 22–23
learning disabilities 15, 18–19, 23

mental disabilities 6, 8, 9, 23
meningitis 12

organizations 28–29

paralysis 8, 16, 25
physical disabilities 6, 8, 17
Pryor, Richard 26

ramps 17, 23
accidents 8

spinal cord 16
sign language 23

tunnel vision 10, 11

wheelchair, use of 8, 15, 16–17, 23, 26, 27